Mastering Rental Properties - How to Create Wealth and Passive Income Through Real Estate Investing

Adidas Wilson

Published by Adidas Wilson, 2018.

MASTERING RENTAL PROPERTIES - HOW TO CREATE WEALTH AND PASSIVE INCOME THROUGH REAL ESTATE INVESTING

First edition. November 13, 2018.

Copyright © 2018 Adidas Wilson.

ISBN: 978-1393700821

Written by Adidas Wilson.

.

Disclaimer

THE AUTHOR HAS MADE every effort to ensure the accuracy of the information within this book was correct at time of publication. The author does not assume and hereby disclaims any liability to any party for any loss, damage, or disruption caused by errors or omissions, whether such errors or omissions result from accident, negligence, or any other cause.

Table of Contents

Introduction

   Ch. 1 - How to Invest in Real Estate

   Ch. 2 - Real Estate Expenses That Blindside Investors

   Ch. 3 - Real Estate Can Make You a Millionaire

   Ch. 4 - How Much Money Does It Take to Invest in Rental Properties?

   Ch. 5 - Rental Property Maintenance Myths

   Ch. 6 - Real Estate is the Best Way to Build Wealth

   Ch. 7 - Buying Rental Property and Becoming a Landlord

   Ch. 8 - Deductions and Record Keeping

   Ch. 9 - How to Quit Your Job in Less Than Six Months

   Ch. 10 - Profitable Rental Property

   Ch. 11 – 10 to 15 Year Plan

   Ch. 12 - House Hacking to Build Real Estate Wealth

   Ch. 13 - Where to Buy an Investment Property – The A, B, C, D Rating System

   Ch. 14 - Single Family Houses Are Your Best Investments

   Ch. 15 - Affordable Housing: Investing for Profit

   Ch. 16 - Buy, Rehab, Rent, Refinance, Repeat Strategy: A Primer for Investors

   Ch. 17 - What Does Cash Flow Mean?

   Ch. 18 - Building a Real Estate Team

   Ch. 19 - Reasons to Invest in Multi-Family Real Estate

   Ch. 20 - Essential Tips for Buying a HUD Home

   Ch. 21 – How to Find a Rental Property in an Expensive Market

   Ch. 22 - Before Investing in Condos

Ch. 23 - Questions to Ask Yourself Before Buying a Fixer-Upper Property

Ch. 24 - Why Passive Investing in Commercial Real Estate is a Smarter Strategy Than Single Family Rentals

Ch. 25 - How to Pick the Ideal Location for Investment Properties

Ch. 26 - Real Estate Financing

Ch. 27 - How to Find Investment Properties

Ch. 28 - Things to Look for When Buying Rental Property

Ch. 29 - The Guide to Making and Accepting an Offer on a Home

Ch. 30 - Closing a Real Estate Deal

Ch. 31 - DIY Landlord: Your Guide to Managing Your Rental

Ch. 32 - Dealing with Problem Tenants

Ch. 33 - 1031 Exchange and Rental Properties

Ch. 34 - Mistakes Inexperienced Landlords Make

Ch. 35 - The Definitive Guide to Using Seller Financing to Buy Real Estate

Conclusion

Introduction

Rental properties are amazing. Other investments like the stock market may be loved by most people but rental properties are superior to them all. Here is why. You can borrow money from someone else or the bank to purchase rental properties and increase the potential profits. This is what is called leverage. Simply put, if you find property you like, you can acquire it without having 100% of the purchase price. In addition to leveraging your cash, you can leverage your abilities and time and do something great. This is not something you can easily do with other forms of investment. With rental properties, you can hustle. You can rehab a property if you want to. If you have networking skills you can leverage them to raise money. If you have the time and skills to look for better deals you can do it as well. When you have rental property, the outcome of your investment depends solely on you. The responsibility to analyze a rental property before purchasing falls on you and so is ensuring that it is in good condition and everything is running properly. The real estate market, just like any other, goes up and down. The beauty of it, however, is that there will always be demand for rental property. This is a long-term investment. This demand is expected to grow over time, thanks to student loans that hinder people from qualifying for mortgages. History has shown that since the beginning of civilization, landlords in every society have amassed wealth by leasing out property. This is still the case today. It is possible for events like the market collapse (2007) to occur. However, rental property investors who invest for the long-term have nothing to worry about. Some experts even argue that those who were keen could predict the 2007 crash. You can choose to invest in small multifamily properties, single-family houses, office buildings, large multifamily apartments and so many other options. There are countless possibilities. Being a rental property investor is not easy, but it is straightforward and fairly simple. There is more to investing in rental properties than just buying and renting. Nevertheless, the strategies are easy to master and there are so many people you can ask. One of the best things about property investing is that you can shop around for a great deal and pay for less than the market value. Insider trading in the stock market is when you make a profit because you had some secret information. This is illegal in the stock market but not in the rental property market.

There are four main profit sources that you can capitalize on:

- Appreciation
- Loan pay down
- Cash flow
- Tax benefits

With property investing, you do not need to be physically present. You can even make money while sleeping.

Chapter 1
How to Invest in Real Estate

Investing in real estate is not complicated, expensive or difficult. There are so many places to put or invest your money such as bonds, stocks, mutual funds, savings, commodities, and real estate, among others. Each form of investment has its advantages and disadvantages. Here, the focus is on real estate investment.

Many people resort to real estate investing mainly because they want financial freedom. Others are in it for the following:

- Tax benefits
- Leverage
- Cash flow
- Depreciation
- Appreciation

The decision and reason for each individual is personal. Just ensure that you are committed before you start. Can You Invest in Real Estate While Holding a Full-Time Job? You can. There are so many kinds of real estate investing, not just what you hear from experts or the TV. The ways to make money are also numerous. Some of the strategies and techniques may be demanding (40 hours a week) and others less demanding (less than 40 hours a year). The length of time you will need to grow your business depends mainly on your personality, investing strategy, timeline and knowledge. Real estate does not have to be your full-time career for you to amass wealth. You can invest on the side. Benefits of Investing While Still Holding Your Full-Time Job. If you keep your day job, you will enjoy some benefits that full-time investors do not. The first benefit is that you do not need to spend the money you make in your investment. If you reinvest all your profits, your business will grow exponentially. Another thing, the stable income of your 9-5 will give you access to long-term financing from banks.

To invest while still maintaining your day job you can:

- Serve as a hard or private money lender
- Buy-and-hold property
- Invest in notes

Do You Need to Pay an Expert to Be Successful?

You do not have to. There are so many investors who have attained success without the help of experts. Most of these gurus just want to sell you the get-rich-quick dream. They prey on desperate people and they can be dangerous. Their main business is to sell you the dream. You can learn a thing or two from gurus but be careful.

Can You Invest in Real Estate if You Have No Money?

It is possible. However, you should understand that every transaction in real estate requires money. You can, therefore invest without using your own money but, other people's money. This is a complex but important strategy. If you have no money, bring something else to the table such as education, connections, time, creativity, and intelligence. A lot of aspiring real estate investors begin their journey by working in the industry first. They earn income while acquiring hands-on education. Here are some real estate careers you can look into:

- Mortgage broker
- Real estate agent
- Title/escrow agent
- Appraiser
- Resident manager
- Project manager
- Construction worker

Some people can make a lot of money in a short period of time—but this is rare. A good real estate investor is patient, persistent, and plans ahead. Aim at growing steadily over time until your dreams and goals are achieved.

Chapter 2

Real Estate Expenses That Blindside Investors

A s you plan to invest in real estate, there are common expenses that you should never forget to take into consideration. However, do you know about the hidden expenses? If you do not include them in your planning, you may be on the losing end.

The Three Big Hidden Expenses

1. Maintenance Expenses

A real estate agent (a doomed one) will estimate the cost of maintenance to be $600 a year for property that rents for $1000 a month. You can be like this agent or be assured that maintenance might never go below 10% of the rent.

1. Management Expenses

Usually, property managers charge 8% to 10% of the rent for property management. Sometimes the amount might be lower, even up to 4% in bigger multifamily apartment situations. For single family homes, never assume less than 10%.

1. Vacancy Expense

A vacancy is inevitable. For a single-family unit, you will either be 100% vacant or 100% full. When accounting for vacancy, 5% is a good number. This ensures that the period between renters is taken care of.

9 More Hidden Expenses That Are Easy to Forget
These may be less common. They are, however, real and have to be paid.

1. Permits and Fees

Many cities are taking advantage of rental licenses to earn some extra cash. This may cost you more than $100 a year.

1. Tenant Screening Charges

There is a cost for screening tenants and you better factor it in. The charge for every adult is about $40 so each rental may cost you $80. You might pass the charge to an incoming tenant.

1. Advertising

In most cases, advertising will be free. Nevertheless, include an expense for a paid ad in case times get slow. For multifamily properties, vacant are common and you might need full-time ads.

1. Evictions

Failure to set aside money for eviction or proper screening may see you become a former landlord. An eviction or bad tenant can cost you years of profit. Always have money to help you recover the cost of a bad tenant.

1. Mileage

You will most likely be doing a lot of driving to your property and the home improvement store. You will also need to drive to show properties, pick up keys, sign leases, answer maintenance calls, empty laundry machines, and clean common areas. Do not ignore this expense.

1. Tools

Decent tools are essential if you plan on taking care of maintenance on your own. Great tools will make the job easier.

1. Banking Charges

Banks will always charge businesses fees. The fee might not be that big, but it needs to be accounted for. Consider check printing fees, cash deposit fees, accounting fees, and bounced check fees.

1. Office Expenses

A good computer is essential in running your business and so is a solid printer. You will need to replace cartridges and buy stamps, paper, envelopes, and labels.

1. Insurance

Property insurance is common knowledge but there is also liability insurance. A liability insurance policy and a business umbrella policy are great investments.

Chapter 3
Real Estate Can Make You a Millionaire

In some cases, working as a team can see you accomplish much more than you would have as an individual. For instance, in Tour de France, cyclists ride ahead of the group in turns to decrease the wind for those at the back. Wolves attack and take down beasts 20 times their size because they hunt in packs. Apart from the above-mentioned teams, there is this other team that is capable of accomplishing great things. It is a team of benefits, not people. A combination of these benefits may be your pathway to all your financial goals. This is about real estate. Real estate is arguably the best form of traditional investing. Nevertheless, purchasing real estate property does not guarantee you riches. To build wealth, you have to capitalize on the wealth generators of this investment. Together, these benefits will make you wealthy. Cash flow is the surplus profit you remain with after paying off all expenses on a property. For instance, if your rental property generates an income of $3,000 and your expenses are $2,500, then your cash flow for the month will be $500. $500 cannot make you a millionaire. However, bear in mind that this is just one of the four wealth generators. Again, probably this $500 is only from one property. With ten units the amount will be $5,000 and $50,000 a month if you own 100 units. This cash flow might help you retire early and wealthy. Appreciation is the natural increase in value of real estate properties. For example, if ten years ago you bought a piece of property for $300,000 and today it is worth $450,000, then you are $150,000 richer, thanks to appreciation. Value does not rise every year and 2007 is a good example. However, history has shown that real estate prices do appreciate over the long term. Just like with cash flow. Appreciation cannot build you immense wealth on its own. It is especially not wise to buy bad deals in the hope that appreciation will bail you out. You have to combine it with the other generators. When you buy your property with a mortgage, you will be paying the lender a certain amount every month. The payment has two parts: interest and principle. The principle is the original amount you borrowed while the interest is the lender's profit. Say you bought a house for $100,000 five years ago and got a mortgage of $80,000 (assume the mortgage was a 30-year one with a 5% fixed rate). The amount you would owe today would be $74,000 only. Ten years from today, you would only owe $65,000. This shows that your equity (difference between the property's worth and what you owe) increased every year. As long as the real estate property appreciated, you would gain value. The U.S government offers tax benefits to investors. The benefits are many and you will enjoy them in different parts of the process.

For example:

- Appreciation and cash flow are not considered self-employment income.
- A deduction (depreciation) often offsets due income tax.
- Profit from the sale of property is taxed at the rate of long-term capital gains or not at all.
- There is a way to defer tax with a 1031 exchange.

Chapter 4

How Much Money Does It Take to Invest in Rental Properties?

How much do you need to invest in rental properties? Most likely less than you think. Many people have allowed their dreams to be crashed by thinking that they do not have the amount it takes to venture into real estate investing. Some people do not know that you do not need to have 100% of the purchase price to invest in real estate. This is where leverage comes in. Some investors can afford to pay the full price of a property using cash but most of investors make use of leverage. In simple terms, leverage is a applying a little effort for great results. In real estate, leverage refers to loans. You, as the borrower, supply a small down payment and the lender pays the rest of the amount for you. Every month, you make a small payment to the lender until the loan is cleared. For instance, for a piece of property worth $200,000, you could only save $40,000 and borrow the rest of the amount from the bank. Despite the fact that you have to make a payment to the bank every month, your income will exceed the loan. Leverage is not all perfect. Using more leverage may mean a greater risk. If you pay the full amount on your own, you will not have the monthly burden of paying off the loan. In that case, if your property is vacant for three months you might still be okay. Also, if you only make a 5% down payment and the property depreciates by 20%, you will be "underwater" and the amount you owe will be bigger than the property's worth. This can be very limiting. So, how should you use leverage? How much should you put down? You can increase your security in certain ways when using leverage. Here are two of the main ways: First, the deal you land is way more important than the down payment. For example, say you buy a piece of property worth $100,000, get a $70,000 loan and only put down 30%. Another investor buys a similar piece of property for $70,000, gets a $70,000 loan and puts 0% down. You will be at a greater risk in this case. Although you owe equal amounts of loans, you have invested more money. Secondly, having enough knowledge while investing in real estate can help you reduce the risk that comes with leverage. If you understand the investment, how to manage it and the market in general, things are likely to go well for you. For a small multi-family house (two to four units), you can get a loan from the bank for as low as 3.5% using the FHA program. You have to live in the house for at least a year, though. Most banks require a minimum down payment of 20% if you qualify for the loan. Real estate investing can go wrong. Cash reserves are important to help you take care of any problems that may arise.

Chapter 5
Rental Property Maintenance Myths

There are a number of rumors surrounding rental repairs and several myths regarding maintenance matters. You cannot avoid performing repair and maintenance services on rental properties. However, the entire ordeal does not have to be a total pain. Here are some common myths:

Myth #1: DIY Repairs Will Save You Money

It is a good thing if you can take care of some of these repairs on your own. If you manage rental property, the skills can be quite useful. If you can do basic stuff like fix appliances or minor plumbing tasks, then there is no need to call a repairman. However, you need to know when to call the right person. Just because you can handle a repair task yourself does not always mean you should. Trying to take care of everything could leave you overwhelmed. Another thing, all that your tenants care about is that the repair be done quickly and conveniently. If you cannot do this, you better hire somebody. Poor maintenance can easily chase away a tenant.

Myth #2: Maintenance and Repairs Should be Left to Tenants

You, the landlord, are physically and financially responsible for the maintenance and repairs, unless it is something such as a light bulb. If the tenant causes the damage they may be responsible; but you will still have to be notified. In this case the tenant may only be financially responsible. In the case of regular, preventive maintenance, the property manager or landlord should handle it—although most people leave it to the residents.

Myth #3: Repairing Vs Replacing

There are two extremes to this myth. There is the optimist who believes that everything can be repaired and there is the other one who insists that it is cheaper to just replace everything. Both of these two extremes are inaccurate. The decision to repair or replace an appliance is dependent on a few factors such as the condition or age of the structure of appliance, previous fixes, safety concerns, and the expected lifetime.

Myth #4: Estimating Maintenance Costs

There are a few formulas that have been suggested to help you estimate the cost of maintenance. See some of them: 50% rule: this one maintains that half of the income will go to operational costs. 1% rule: maintenance will take up about 1% of the property value per year. Square footage formula: for every square foot set aside $1 for yearly maintenance. 5x rule: the yearly maintenance cost will be 1.5 times the amount of monthly rate. Murphy's Law: if anything can go wrong, it will.

Estimating the amount, you will spend on maintenance is great but there are way too many variables. Whichever formula you choose, know that the actual costs will most likely exceed your expectations.

Myth #5: What Do Security Deposits Cover?

Here are two common deposits surrounding security deposits: Tenant misunderstanding: the security deposit is rent for the last month. Unless the landlord and tenant agree on this, it should not be assumed. Landlord misunderstanding: the security deposit is for between vacancy cleaning and repair costs. The purpose of the security deposit is to perform repairs on damages caused by the tenant (not normal wear and tear) and cover unpaid rent.

Chapter 6
Real Estate is the Best Way to Build Wealth

A certain real estate investor, Dana Bull, got into real estate investing at a very young age. In her early 20s, she bought and rented out a condo to earn some extra cash, making her a young landlord. She currently owns a number of rentals. She says that, just like any other business, real estate investing takes hard work and patience. When Dana was 22 years old, she started a business "accidentally". She convinced her boyfriend and together they bought a condo. She had no idea that that would be the first step to a great career in real estate. All throughout their 20s, they bought more properties in Boston. Later on, they got married. Speaking honestly, Dana says that the entire investment thing was not a walk in the park. There was a lot to be done and sacrifices to be made. It is when things got tough in the beginning that she reminded herself to focus on the prize. Why is real estate investing worthwhile? Cash flow: investors love rental properties because they have the potential of generating positive cash flow. After paying off all the expenses, you will be left with profit. Some people are even choosing to rent out an extra room or space in their primary residence for some extra money. Appreciation: this is not always the case, but more often than not, housing values appreciate over time. Your property will be worth more after some time. This is why real estate is considered the ultimate nest egg. Leverage: this advantage is not very well known. If you consistently pay down the mortgage, you may tap the built-up equity. This is a great rainy-day fund. With multiple properties, you can cash out whenever you want. Tax advantages: unlike regular homeowners, landlords have some extra advantages. They can deduct items such as maintenance, depreciation, insurance, and interest. Moreover, when you sell your property and exercise a 1031 exchange and the proceeds go into reinvesting in a new property, you can defer capital-gains taxes. The best thing about real estate investing is that you have the freedom to create your own strategy. Dana, for instance, buys small multifamily properties (3-4 units each). She says that this strategy is best for those that want to live in one unit and rent out the rest. Real estate investing is no different from any other business and that means that it is not easy. Understand the following: Getting started is difficult: this venture requires money, time, or both. These two resources are not easy to spare. Scaling is even more difficult: owning property will not make it easier. There will be challenges and situations on the way and you have to face them head on. Waiting is the most difficult: slow-and-steady always wins the race. The journey to your goals may be long and full of obstacles. Create a great strategy. Your business model should be reliable for the long-run.

Chapter 7

Buying Rental Property and Becoming a Landlord

Do you see yourself owning property someday? Before you pick up the phone to call a real estate agent, understand what you are getting yourself into. To start earning income right away you will have to rent out the property. It sounds easy but there are downsides to it. Potential landlords always take into consideration the cost of buying a piece of property; however, many of them completely overlook the remodeling costs. If the house you are buying is out-of-date or damaged, the cost of making it rentable could be significant. A house in good condition may also require a few touches. There are strict requirements that rental properties have to meet according to the law before they can be rented out. When you consider all the costs you will realize that you need much more than just the purchasing amount. Repairs are inevitable for a landlord. Serious repairs need urgent attention—otherwise you may incur extra damage costs. Repairs are sudden, and they often require a lot of money. Some tenants will only call you when there is a major problem while others will call you for every little problem. You have to be prepared for everything. There are tenants who have no issues paying rent on time. These are the perfect tenants. Others are good and will inform you ahead of time that they may be a little late in paying. Then there are those who neither pay nor call. This calls for some bill collection skills. Before you become a landlord ask yourself if you can confront tenants and make judgment calls. In most cases, your tenants will be great; paying rent on time, respecting neighbors and taking good care of the property. However, at some point you will have to deal with problem causing tenants. These tenants may not pay rent on time. Other times they will fight with other tenants and they may cause damage to your property. All these are problems you will have to solve. If you look at the landlord and tenant laws, evictions appear to be simple. In reality, they are tedious and costly. Even if the process goes smoothly, you cannot avoid losing a lot of money and time. When a tenant does not renew their lease, you are left with a vacant house. In bad times it may stay empty for a few months. A successful landlord will consider good and bad times when managing finances. When the units are occupied, with tenants paying rent on time, remember to save for when things will not be as great. You can easily be sued if a tenant gets injured on your property. Even with homeowner's insurance, you need to always have your property in good condition. Understand your area's safety codes and adhere to them. Make the effort to check your property regularly. While filing taxes, you need to report the income from your rental property. Many landlords usually overlook property tax. Remember if you are a homeowner with a rental house you might have to pay double of what you were paying as property tax before you bought the rental increased. Do not take the issue of taxes lightly.

Chapter 8

Deductions and Record Keeping

A s a rental estate owner, you have federal tax responsibilities that you should know of. You have to report all your rental income. Associated expenses are usually deducted. A cash basis taxpayer is supposed to report their rental income for the year they receive it. It does not matter when they earned it. In the same way, expenses are deducted in the same year they are paid. With the accrual method, instead of reporting income when you receive it, you report when it is earned, and expenses are deducted when they are incurred, not when they are paid. Your gross income is the entire amount you get as rent. This is any amount you earn for occupation or use of your property. In addition to this, there are other payments that may be considered rental income and have to be reported. One example is advance rent. It should be included in the year it is received, regardless of the period it was supposed to cover—it does not matter what accounting method you are using. A security deposit is advance rent since it usually caters for the last month's rent. If, according to the agreement with your tenant, you are supposed to return it when the lease ends, do not include it in your income. However, if your tenant violates some terms and you end up keeping all or part of the deposit, you need to report what you keep in that year. If a tenant offers you a payment to cancel the lease, that payment is considered rent and you have to report it in the year it is received regardless of the accounting method. If a tenant pays your expenses, these payments should be included in the rental income. If the expenses are deductible you can deduct them. Instead of money, you receive services or property as rent, you must include them as the fair market value in the income. You can deduct a few rental expenses when filing your taxes. These expenses include property tax, depreciation, repairs, mortgage interest, and operating expenses. You can deduct some of the necessary and ordinary expenses for maintaining, conserving, and managing your property. Necessary expenses are the appropriate ones such as advertising, taxes, utilities, insurance, and interest. Ordinary expenses are the general and common ones. The cost of certain repairs, materials, maintenance, and supplies used to keep the property in good condition can be deducted. Deductible expenses paid by a tenant can be deducted. The cost of improvements is not deductible. It can, however, be recovered through depreciation. For real estate such as apartments, buildings or rooms, you report on Form 1040, Schedule E, Part I. Good records are useful in monitoring the progress of your investment, know the source of receipts, prepare tax returns, and financial statements, support reported items and monitors deductible expenses. Keep all the documents that support your reports.

Chapter 9

How to Quit Your Job in Less Than Six Months

Y ou probably do not love your job. Statistics have shown that a majority of people are not happy at their jobs. What can you do to quit your job? Real estate investing can help you get away from your miserable job and still have a steady stream of income. It is not an easy thing to do and you will not succeed overnight. You will have to commit and persist. Quitting your job is not a decision that you should make without thinking it through. Real estate investing is a job too. You will encounter jerks and a lot of pressure, just as you do at your current job. You will be happy having a real estate investing career if you really love real estate investing. Otherwise, you can still invest in real estate without necessarily having a career in real estate. There are so many ways that you can use to make money in real estate. Here are a few. When you decide to quit your job, you do not have to invest in real estate—you can get a real estate career instead. This is an amazing way to make income as you learn the ropes of the business.

Some of the most common jobs include:

- Mortgage broker
- Property manager
- Real estate agent
- Escrow officer
- Home remodeling contractor
- Title company employee
- Marketing professional

- Live-in resident manager

Real estate wholesaling entails finding a great deal on real estate property, putting it under legal contract and selling the contract to someone else. This method is good for beginner investors because it is fairly simple. You will still need to put in a lot of work and skills. House flipping involves buying cheap homes, fixing them, and reselling them to investors. The profits can be significant with this method. Buy-and-Hold cash flow investing, you have to collect a substantial amount of positive cash flow income properties. It is a little difficult and requires a lot of money. Honest evaluation: where are you at in life? Thoroughly evaluate yourself and your situation. Collect as much information as you can. Talk to seasoned investors and ask all the right questions. Clearly identify your new source of income: what exactly do you want to do? Outline your objective: what is your goal? Create a detailed plan: now that you have a goal, how are you going to achieve it? Include all the details. Reduce your expenses: it is a big deal to quit your job. The financial consequences will not be light. There are sacrifices you will have to make as you venture into self-employment. Save up some cushion money: before you quit your job, have some money saved up for emergencies and capital. Life will not get easier when you quit your job. Networking is crucial: start networking because you will need other people. Now you can hand in your two weeks' notice.

Chapter 10
Profitable Rental Property

If you aspire to make money from rental property as a first-time investor, the idea can be a little intimidating. The business is not easy and has so many challenges. What should you look for in an income property? You may be tempted to engage the help of a real estate agent in the process of buying property. However, it is advisable that you conduct this search on your own. The pressure from an agent could make you buy something that you are really not comfortable with. Check out all the options that fit your investing range. This range is determined by whether you want to hire a property manager or manage the property yourself. If you want to manage it yourself, it is wise to look for something near your own home; otherwise, the distance is not a problem. The neighborhood hugely influences your vacancy rates and the type of tenants you are likely to get. If the property is near a university, most of your tenants will be students and you will have to face vacancies regularly. Property taxes vary, and as an investor you need to know how much you will be paying. In some instances, high property taxes are not necessarily bad, especially if it is a great neighborhood with the potential of long-term tenants. Consult homeowners in the area or visit the municipality's assessment office for tax information. If you want to invest in family-sized property, assess the quality of educational facilities around. Poor schools or none at all, will affect your investment. Everyone wants to live in a safe place. Instead of asking the one who is selling you the property, go to the library or the police and get the correct information on crime rates. People are always moving to areas with increasing employment opportunities and that means more tenants.

Visit your local library or the U.S Bureau of Labor Statistics to get this information. See if the neighborhood has parks, movie theaters, gyms, public transport hubs, malls, and other facilities that renters look for. Development means that an area is growing. Check the municipal planning department for anything that is coming up. When the number of listings is high in a neighborhood, something could be wrong, or it could just be a seasonal cycle. Make sure you know what it is. The same applies to high vacancy rates. Check the average rent in the area and make the necessary calculations. See if you will have any income left after paying off the expenses. An area prone to flooding or earthquakes may eat away your income through insurance. As you talk to homeowners in the area, make sure you consult the renters as well. They are more likely to be honest. Make several visits to know what the neighborhood is like. Beginners are advised to start with single-family homes. They are low maintenance and likely to attract long term tenants. Consider the projected cash flow and appreciation potential of the property. Also consider the cost of repairs and maintenance.

Chapter 11
10 to 15 Year Plan

When you have the capital, rental property investments can be rewarding. But even with little money, making one million dollars is possible. The more money you have saved up for investment in rentals, the easier it will be for you to make $1 million. This plan is going to assume that the potential investor earns $75,000 and they are able to save 10% of their salary. $75,000 may not seem like much since you need more money to buy rental properties. Lucky for you, there are ways through which you can buy investment properties with less money. In your first year as an investor, you are better off buying a REO or HUD home. It may require some work, but it will qualify for a conventional or FHA loan. Purchasing properties below market value is a good strategy and with REO or HUD homes, you can do that. Suppose these homes cost $100,000. First, you need to purchase a house. Buy it as an owner-occupied and turn it into a rental later on. For instant equity, look for a great deal. The best way to get this deal is to purchase a house that requires repairs. In the case of a HUD home, $5000 of the repairs can be rolled into the loan so you will only have to put down 3.5%. If a lot of money will be required for the repairs, roll the extra money into the loan using an FHA 203K loan. In this case, assume that the house will need $4,000 in work for a loan qualification and you purchased a HUD home— the costs are rolled into the loan. Now, an FHA loan requires you to pay monthly mortgage insurance and a mortgage insurance premium upfront (the estimated cost is $200+ a month). The mortgage insurance for a conventional loan is much lower than that of FHA. Nevertheless, it may not be possible to roll repairs into the loan. Before closing, ask the seller to make some repairs. For cosmetic repairs, you can get a loan before closing without having to make the repairs. The estimated amount you will need to close on this hypothetical property is about $5,000. Because repairs were needed, and it was a foreclosure, the amount is below the market value. Once the repair is done, it's worth will be around $125,000. If you buy the home as an owner occupant, you must live in it for no less than one year. After the first year, you will gain $22,000, give or take, in net worth— that is, $125,000 minus $100,000 (purchase price) minus $4,000 (repairs) plus $1,000 received in equity pay down. Remember that you did not collect any rent in the first year because you occupied it as the owner to receive a lower down payment. In the second year, you can rent this house and purchase another owner-occupied house with the same strategy. If you purchase the house immediately, you cannot count the first house's rent as income right away. For this to work, try to purchase homes priced very low so that you qualify for two homes at the same time. Otherwise, you will have to wait about a year before the rent counts as income. For FHA mortgage you can only get one at a time. So, in this case you will have to opt for a conventional loan (5% down). In year two, you will have saved up another $7,500 from your salary and you will have an extra $2,500 from year one. The total will be $11,500. The second home will cost $100,000. The seller will pay 3% closing costs. For the second house you will need $5,000 for down payment and $5,000 in repairs. The total cost will be $10,000 for an owner-occupied house. The repaired value will be $125,000. Say you rent the first home for $1,300 a month and taxes and insurance eat up $550. If you factor in maintenance, vacancy, and mortgage insurance, the positive cash flow could be $300 a month. In year two, you earned $25,000 from purchasing the second home (equity) and $3,600 from cash flow. You also earned $2,500 (equity pay down for the two loans). In the second year, you used all of year one's savings, but you made $3,600 (cash flow) and saved up $7,500. The total is $11,100. Using an owner-occupied loan and $10,000 cash, buy another home. Your net worth rises to $53,000 after you have added equity gained for the new home, equity pay down and cash flow. Again, you rent the second home. In the fourth year, you buy another home below market value. Your cash flow will increase to $7,200 a year. Add to that $7,500 in savings and $1,100 previous savings. You will have a total of $17,300 saved up. From this amount, subtract $10,000 for a new house. Your net worth has now increased $25,000 plus $4,500 (equity pay down). Your total net worth has increased $90,800 in four years. You have four homes, three of which are rented out. You can remove the mortgage insurance at this point for the conventional loan, but this plan will not do that. In year five, repeat the same process to get the following numbers. Your cash flow is now at $10,800, $5,800 previous savings and $7,500 saved up. The total is $25,600. If you buy another home, you will use $10,000 and remain with $15,600. Your net worth increases $10,800 cash flow, $25,000 for buying a new house and $7,000 for equity pay down making a total of $133,600. It may be difficult to get four houses but since you are buying them as an owner-occupant, the loan is easier to get. In the sixth year, repeat the same process. Previous cash will be $14,100, cash flow of $14,400 and $7,500 in savings. The total will be $37,500 then subtract $10,000 for a new house. In your account you will have $27,500 left. Your equity increases to $13,500, added to $25,000 from the purchase and $14,400 in cash flow. Your total net worth increases by $186,500. Buy the seventh home. In the bank you will have $26,000 (previous savings), $18,000 (cash flow) and $7,500 (new savings). The total is $53,000. This year, you can purchase two houses, an investor-owned and an owner-occupied. For the investment property you will need to put a minimum of 20% down and money for repairs. Since you will still buy below market value, it is assumed that you will add $25,000 and $3,600 in equity and cash flow respectively. For down payment and repairs you will spend about $32,000 for the investment property. After buying two houses, you will be left with $11,000. Your net worth increases by $60,500 making it $247,000. In the eighth year, you buy two properties. After adding equity pay down, increased cash flow and the extra homes, your net worth increases by $98,000 in a year making your total net worth $345,000. After buying a house (owner-occupant) in year eight, you will remain with $42,200. You will be able to acquire another investment property but don't.

Even while making $75,000 a year, your net worth will increase by $100,000 in a single year. In year nine you will add $26,500 (equity pay down), $25,000 (equity with purchases) and $28,200 (cash flow) making an increase of $80,300 in net worth. Over the nine years, you will have increased your net worth by $425,500. After buying another house you will be left with savings worth $60,000. You can purchase another home and still have $26,500 left. In the tenth year, you can purchase two more houses and remain with $28,000. Your net worth goes up by $114,500 making a total of $540,000. In the eleventh year, you can purchase two more homes and boost your net worth by $129,000 making a total of $669,200. At this point your cash flow is $43,000 a year and after buying two houses you will have $36,700 left. If you want, you can even purchase a third one. In the twelfth year, with $94,000 available, buy three homes if you want. If you decide to buy three houses, you will have $22,000 left in savings, $44,500 equity paid down and cash flow amounting to $50,400. Your net worth is $814,000. Because in the twelfth year you purchased three homes, the thirteenth year your net worth has increased by $190,000 and your net worth is $1,004,300. Your cash flow is $61,200 a year. You have also paid $54,000 of equity. You have 16 rental houses giving you more than $60,000 a year.

Variables Not Included in the Plan

- Inflation: it may cause wages, rents and prices of homes to increase.
- Taxes: the issue of tax can be complicated.
- Refinancing: you can easily refinance some properties and be able to acquire more but that was not factored in.
- It is difficult to get a loan more than four times.

- It may be unrealistic to buy owner-occupied houses every year.
- It is assumed that you manage your properties yourself.

Chapter 12
House Hacking to Build Real Estate Wealth

Owning your own home can help you achieve your goals if you want to build wealth. House hacking is when you rent out your home. You can rent out a spare bedroom, a part of your multi-unit property, or live with a roommate. How do you get started with house hacking? Real estate investing can be intimidating for young people because of the 20-25% down payment required to get a loan. However, with house hacking, a tiny down payment can work. If you qualify for USDA or VA, you have a great advantage. You can get away with 0% down payment although their upfront fees are high. Other options include a conventional mortgage and FHA loans. Not all houses are "hackable" in equal measures. When buying a multi-family home, ensure that it will still be able to meet cash flow needs should you decide to move. Having roommates so you can cut down on expenses is a great idea but having negative-cash flow will not help much. It is not financially impossible for most people, but it is socially impossible. You need to be flexible and trust people. However, think of the financial benefits. You will save so much on the mortgage. Even people with families (including kids) can successfully house hack. House hacking requires money. Save up money while living in the house. When you move out you should be able to convert the property into a cash-flowing rental. Consider the following calculations before venturing into house hacking. According to the 1% rule, the gross rent of a rental property should be equal to 1% of the value of each property every month. If a house is worth $200,000, the fair-market rent should not be less than $2,000 per month. With you living in the property, the 1% rule is not that significant. Evaluate the house as though you are renting it all out. The 1% may seem impossible. In this case, consider multi-family rental properties. You will have a higher chance of earning more income compared to the value of the house. If you want to rent it out on Airbnb, be realistic in your estimate. You cannot assume that you will have visitors every day of the month, each paying the full price. If the property passes the 1% test, see it will have a positive net operating income. This is what you can expect after paying the mortgage. When calculating your cap rate, factor in the idea that you will be living in the house as well. The cap rate you want to attain depends on your goals. If you love the cap rate, it is time to decide whether or not the house is perfect for house hacking. First, calculate the yearly cash flow based on the amount you expect tenants or roommates to pay as rent. The result may be negative. Now, calculate the cash flow based on what you would receive if you were not living in the house (imputed cash flow).

Chapter 13

Where to Buy an Investment Property – The A, B, C, D Rating System

There are so many decisions that a real estate investor has to make other than where to buy property. You need to understand the criteria for choosing the best investment locations. You can make money in any of the classes depending on your financial goals and real estate niche. Read or listen on to find out how this grading system works. When you hear people talk about these classes, they could be referring to the property or location. A C property could be in an A location. This rating system is subjective. Class A property refers to the best. As for a location, it refers to the most desirable parts of town—the ones in high demand. For instance, in a college town, Class A locations (the most desirable) are the ones close to recreational areas and campus. The faculty or students can bike or walk to campus and still be close to the recreational area. Although the distance matters a lot, there are other factors to consider. A Class A building, in most cases, is a remodeled or brand new one with no functional problems. For apartment buildings it includes luxury amenities. Class B locations is an attractive location but not the best. Tenants are well-off, but they do not have expensive taste. In the case of the college town example, a Class B location is a little bit further from the downtown commercial district and campus. This location has attractive features as well but is not as luxurious as a Class A location. Class B buildings are newer or well-kept buildings with fancy finishes here and there. They are very attractive and fairly priced. Class B buildings have less impressive amenities. A Class C location is generally a working-class neighborhood. There are both owner-occupied and rental properties. The rental rates in these areas are below average. A Class B building is older and may require some improvements and repairs. Although the building is a little worn out, it is still great for living in. Mobile homes also fit in this category. They depreciate very quickly. When buying a Class C building, do not underestimate the cost of repairs. Class D locations are a lot more like Class C and defining them can be a little difficult. The tenants in Class D locations are low income earners. These locations are characterized by high crime rates. Class D buildings are old and require a lot of work. Sometimes they may not be livable. However, they have the potential of making you a lot of money. You can buy a Class D building in a Class A, B, or C location and fix it. The details in the definitions above are from one investor. Other investors may have different opinions. The collective opinion of investors creates trends such as cap rates. Comparing these cap rates will enable you to know which location is the best.

Chapter 14

Single Family Houses Are Your Best Investments

John Schaub, a real estate teacher, has been in the real estate investing business for 32 years. He only buys houses and not shopping centers or apartments. According to him, houses are a far better investment because they require less work and make more money. John always advises people to invest in single-family houses. Here are seven reasons why no investment can beat single family houses. Houses can be referred to as an unusual investment also known as a hybrid investment. They are a source of rental income. However, their retail value is not directly affected by that rental income. An apartment building with 10 units, for instance, increases or decreases in value depending on the amount of net rent produced. A vacant house that is well cared for will increase in value just like an occupied one because buyers of houses care about the condition of the house and the neighborhood. Even when the real estate market is bad, a banker will prefer to loan money against a single-family house instead of stock portfolio or a commercial property. Houses are fairly stable and hold their value in most cases. There are also more buyers looking for houses than other real estate properties. Vacancies tend to be shorter because there is a high demand for residences. Usually, when buying a house, you do not deal with a full-time professional investor. The ones that are out to make a profit and have great negotiation skills. A regular homeowner, on the other hand, could just be selling to solve a problem. There are always people selling houses. People move, pass away, divorce, start families, and retire every day. In any town, you will always find more family houses than any other real estate property. Because of this, deals never run out. Compared with mobile homes, apartments, and lower end houses, tenants of homes in great neighborhoods are more likely to pay on time and be self-sufficient. For an investor that values their time, this factor is important. Diversification is a key principle in investing. Things could go wrong and that will be fatal if all your eggs are in one basket. Having single family houses helps you spread out your capital among various deals in various neighborhoods. For instance, using the same amount that it would take to purchase a 10-unit apartment in one location, you can diversify and buy houses in different neighborhoods. Retail and all cash when you sell is probably the most attractive thing about single family houses. The federal government aims at subsidizing the housing market. For this reason, there are so many loans available to enable buyers to acquire houses and pay you in cash. It is much more difficult to get all cash for something such as a commercial building or home park. In a free market, an investor can do business however they like, and it will still work. This is just one way.

Chapter 15
Affordable Housing: Investing for Profit

A seasonal real estate investor is more than just a landlord. He is a shrewd business executive. He is like business and portfolio managers who, in the process of maximizing profit, create value for their clients. This chapter talks about investing in affordable housing. People with disabilities and seniors: a big percentage of the U.S population is made up of older people (65+) and people with disabilities. According to research, the numbers are expected to rise significantly in the next 20-30 years. These people require houses that make their day-to-day lives easier (such as ramps and wheelchair accessible bathrooms). Off-campus housing for students: the increasing number of non-traditional and adult college and university students has made the demand for off-campus housing rise. International students and adult students require private housing. Off-base housing for military: there are both on and off base housing options for military service members. Off-base housing should offer convenience in terms of distance and ease of moving in and out. Anyone interested in investing in military housing should learn about federal contracting and the specific guidelines of service branches. Re-entry and rehabilitation programs: group homes for adults and children, halfway houses for newly released ex-convicts and recovering addicts and transitional houses for homeless families and people should be neighborhood-based. Investors should take affordability seriously because it determines marketability and profitability. Subsidized housing programs allow low-income earners to afford rent. Find out the median income for the neighborhood. You can get that information from the U.S Census Bureau and real estate websites. 30% of the median income is what you can expect as your gross income for every affordable rental unit. First, know your operating expenses. If you have rental units, start by factoring in insurance and taxes. Include utilities, maintenance, transfer costs, and any other fees. For sale units, know your closing costs at the time of buying and at the time of selling, financing costs, transfer costs, labor, and material costs for rehabilitation or construction. For both sale and rental units, determine your advertising and marketing costs. To determine your income from rental units, take the gross income expected from each affordable unit. For income from sale units, take the purchase price. Next use the formula: income – expenses = gross profit. Consider income tax and depreciation as they will both affect your cash flow. Make sure you get units that qualify for rental subsidies. For sale units, try to minimize rehabilitation and construction costs.

- Use simple logic. If a unit is not profitable, then it is definitely not marketable and vice versa.
- Capitalize on foreclosed homes.
- Consult with agencies that buy properties below market value and resell after rehabilitating.
- Talk to a realtor and acquire knowledge about the local FSBO (for sale by owner) market.

All successful real estate investors know how and when to move according to changes in the market. Research extensively on financing options available to real estate investors. Consult a local mortgage broker or banker to know about lender programs. Also join investor associations and network.

Action Plan

- Stay informed.
- Be involved.
- Become a profitable investor.

Chapter 16

Buy, Rehab, Rent, Refinance, Repeat Strategy: A Primer for Investors

The BRRRR real estate investing method was coined by Brandon Turner and analyzed. A good purchase is a part of all good deals. When buying a house that you plan on holding, it is important to remember that a great feedback mechanism does not exist. When you receive an appraisal, you have every right to disagree with it. You will encounter homeowners who believe that their property is worth a crazy price. In the case of flipping, your profit or loss after the sale will show you how well you did. When holding properties, you may end up thinking that the appraisal was not that good. Buy and hold investors have a tendency of getting lazy. The BRRRR method is meant to help you get back all the money you invested in a house when you refinance. Flippers have a 70% rule which is great. Holders may go for 75%. There are things that are not necessary unless you are working on luxury rentals. They will cost a lot. They include bay windows, hot tubs, granite countertops, chandeliers, and Brazilian hardwood floors, among others. Finishing a garage or basement for rentals is also not worth it in most cases. However, refinishing hardwoods, adding tile, and two-tone paint may be worth it. Everything in the house should be functional and in good shape. You will not benefit much from being a slumlord. Put a little more effort to the front of the property. A poor first impression has the ability to sink an appraisal. Banks are usually reluctant to refinance an unoccupied house, so you should prioritize renting. Screening is very important because you want great tenants. It also helps with financing. Appraisers may or may not care about the pleasantness and cleanliness of the tenant. Notify your tenant in advance that you will be doing an appraisal. Remind them again the day before so they can do the necessary cleaning. It is not a must for them to be present, though. Nowadays, it is easier to find a bank that can refinance a single-family property. That was not always the case. However, even if things are better now, you still need to ask a few questions. Do they pay off debt only or they offer cash out? Move on if they do not offer cash out. What is their seasoning period? The BRRRR method works best when you borrow on the value appraised. look for banks that do that. When you find one, impress them and make them come to a decision quickly. Give them enough information and be as clear as possible. Rinse and repeat. When the BRRRR strategy is done properly, you will have a cash-flowing rental property for nothing or very little down. It is an awesome way—and most experts swear by it. They say it is the best way to amass wealth in the real estate industry.

Chapter 17
What Does Cash Flow Mean?

The words "positive cash flow" are music to real estate investor's ears. Cash flow is the amount of money that is coming in. When the number is positive, the money that is coming in is more than what is going out. Money continuously flowing in is one of the reasons why real estate is so attractive to investors. Real estate investing is among the few investments that offer a steady stream of income without having to sell products or look for new customers. Flippers (those who buy damaged houses, renovate and resell them) do not depend on cash flow but equity gain. In rental real estate, there are several sources of positive cash flow including:

- Deposits for cleaning and security
- Rent
- Unexpected gains from surrendered deposits, late fees, and check fees
- Fees for background and credit checks

Expenses associated with owning real estate properties often offset these gains. They include:

- Monthly payments for HOA (homeowner association) fees, maintenance, repairs, utilities and PITI (principle, interest, taxes and insurance)
- Losses due to unforeseen vacancies, accidents, theft, fires or weather
- Incidental costs from property visits, management and

marketing

It is not a guarantee, but a property can start generating positive cash flow on the day you acquire it. The greatest way to build wealth in rental real estate is to buy low and rent high. Newbie investors no longer rely on beginner's luck. They have opted for turnkey property management groups for lucrative opportunities. Choosing the best properties is both an art and science. Local market conditions affect real estate and so it is wise to consult with experts of specific locations. Acquire as much knowledge as you can from them so you can learn the most suitable way to increase your cash flow. Home prices change and so does rent and neighborhood characteristics. In addition to being experienced with the target market of your property, you need to monitor the local conditions, so you can set fair rental rates. Tax laws favor rental housing ownership so try and understand how everything works. Your tax advisor or property manager can guide you on the best approach. There are two approaches; accrual and cash system (provided the annual receipts are not more than $5 million). The accrual system involves recording payments and income before they are made. You can commit a verbal commitment to pay rent as cash. The cash system shows the actual amount of cash you have at a certain time. The cash approach works best if you want the reading of your cash flow to be accurate. If you are above $5 million you have to use the accrual approach. With the accrual system, you should be careful not to treat paperwork balances as cash. Cash flow is an essential component of any company or business, from small real estate investors to large corporations. If you keep it positive your income stream will increase, and you will, in turn, have more investment options.

Chapter 18
Building a Real Estate Team

An amazing real estate team is better than an amazing individual agent any day. Here is advice from top realtors on team building. Scott Parker, a sales manager at John Greene Realtor advises investors to read the book E-Myth by Michael Berger. He says that many agents do not understand that when growing a team, you will have to be a manager, entrepreneur, and technician, all at the same time. You can only scale by having processes and systems in place. Bruce Ailion, an associate broker and attorney at RE/Max Town and Country says that you need to find quality teammates. A test like the DISC testing helps you know whether or not potential teammates have the skillset needed to boost sales. Lori Ballen is a realtor and digital marketing strategist based in Las Vegas. She says that you should create a team when there is need. Add more team members if you can afford it and if they are needed. Bryan David is a broker at Bryan David Group. His best advice to you is that you should be consistent in your process. He uses the Keller Personality Assessment method. Tim and Julie Harris are real estate coaches. They say that your business should be systemized first. This way, the team can work smoothly without having to ask questions about every procedure. Emile L'Eplattenier is a real estate analyst at FitSmallBusiness.com. He says that a virtual assistant will help you with daily social media and administrative tasks; which will give you an easier time in your recruiting process. Mike Higgings, a Green Bay realtor at Caleb Hayes Real Estate Group says that apart from talent, the personality of your team members should fit into their roles. Greg McDaniel is a host of Real Estate Uncensored and a realtor. He talks about the ideal team structure in a

YouTube video. Anthony Marguleas is a broker at Almafi Estates. He says that building a team is not that hard and you have no reason to wait. Joshua Jarvis is a realtor at Jarvis Team Realty. He says that no matter how talented someone is, do not give them a role they are not suited for. Negar Souza is a realtor at Niroomad & Souza Team. She says that you should hire members that have the skills you lack. Ben Ganje is a realtor at Ganje + Neumann. He says that delegation is a powerful tool. Stan Jones is a realtor at Stan Jones Team. He says that you should invest in people. Learn about your team members and their needs. Mike Higgins says that you should have a model and a plan to guide you as you grow. Tim and Julie Harris say that even when you hire people, you should stay around and oversee what is going on. Lori Ballen says that you should learn all about real estate models before you start hiring.

Chapter 19

Reasons to Invest in Multi-Family Real Estate

Some investors cannot deal with the very volatile stock market and they, therefore, find real estate to be a great investment alternative. It also works well for investors who want to actively grow their capital rather than have their money in a fund under someone else's management. Real estate investing is awesome because there are so many strategies that you can successfully employ. Take Zhang Xin and Donald Bren, for instance. They are both real estate moguls who became billionaires by developing different commercial and residential properties. Sam Zell, Equity Residential founder, built his wealth slowly via an income producing portfolio of rentals. There are many other real estate investors who have become wealthy through house flipping. Investing in rental properties is a great investment for people who would like an extra source of income and in addition, a slow and steady appreciation of portfolio value. In residential real estate, you can invest in two major types of properties: multifamily and single family. A single-family property consists of only one renting unit while a multifamily property (apartment complex) has a number of rentable spaces. Investing in multifamily properties is not that easy but it has its advantages. See these three reasons why you should consider multifamily real estate instead of single family real estate. Single family homes are usually cheaper that multi-family homes when you are buying for investment purposes. Because of this, investors think that it is harder to get a loan for a multifamily property than it is to get financing for a single-family property. What they do not know is that banks are more likely to approve a loan for a multifamily property because such properties are consistent in generating monthly cash flow. Having a few vacancies or some tenants paying rent late does not stop the cash flow. In the case of a single-family unit, when a tenant moves out the property becomes 100% vacant. Another thing, single-family rentals have higher chances of a foreclosure. A multifamily property, therefore, poses less risk for the lender. If you want your rental units' portfolio to grow, investing in multifamily properties is a good option. An apartment building with 20 units is better than 20 single family homes in different locations in terms of ease of management and time saving. Sometimes, you will need to have separate loans for each of the 20 single family homes which can be hectic. With one or two single family properties, hiring a property manager is not a wise thing to do financially because of the small portfolio. Multi-family properties, on the other hand, bring in more money and the investor can comfortably enjoy the services of a property manager. There are many strategies that you can use in real estate investing and still become successful. Investing in multifamily homes has a lot of advantages such as the ability to employ a property manager, better access to financing, and better chances of growing your rental portfolio.

Chapter 20
Essential Tips for Buying a HUD Home

HUD homes were not that much of a hot topic in 2006 when the housing boom peaked. However, a housing bust followed making the HUD program a household name. A HUD home is basically a program by the U.S Department of Housing and Urban Development. The government acquires HUD homes owing to foreclosures on FHA-insured mortgages. HUD aims at selling these homes to regain the monetary loss. During the recession, many people lost their homes giving foreclosure a negative connotation. However, purchasing a HUD home can be a great deal and an awesome experience. It helps to understand the HUD program and the foreclosure process. Many people who want to buy HUD homes are not usually familiar with the entire concept, so do not feel alone. The first thing you need to do is explore the available official information on these homes. Remember that it is a government program and it has government rules. There is, however, a lot of information on the department's website and it features frequently asked questions. In addition, you will find state-specific information and tips on inspections and loans. At times, investors consider HUD homes gold mines. They see a huge potential for profit in flipping or renting them out. This means that you will be competing with seasoned investors who have access to capital. According to the law, when a home first hits the market, HUD does not accept any bids within the first 30 days. You will find HUD homes listed on several realty sites like Re/Max Holdings Inc. and Trulia Inc. The most updated and comprehensive site is the government-run one, hudhomestore.com. If you are thinking about involving a realtor, they should be registered with HUD; otherwise, they cannot represent you. It is very important to buy a property with feasible interest rates and mortgage payments. There are online mortgage calculators that can help you figure out how much monthly mortgage you can afford to pay and any other factors that have an influence on your purchase. Window shopping is okay but secure financing in time. Many buyers have lost their ideal homes to other buyers because of delayed loan approval. When you talk to mortgage lenders, make sure you are thoroughly informed. The two best options include the 203(K) rehab and renovation loan and the $100 down payment program. Read everything you can about the home's history such as recent tax assessments, average sale price of similar homes, and sales history. In your research do not neglect addendums to the property. There is a lot of legally mandated information that you cannot ignore—for instance, your dream home was probably a meth lab. There are states that require a seller, by law, to inform a buyer whether or not the property was used in production of meth. If the state you are shopping in does not have that requirement, do your own air quality audit. If a home was used as a meth lab, getting an FHA loan might be difficult. Make sure you complete the inspection before you make an offer.

Chapter 21

How to Find a Rental Property in an Expensive Market

Investors venture into real estate hoping for long-term passive income. Rental income is capable of providing consistent passive income, but real estate investment can be risky. Buying at the wrong time may cause you to lose a significant amount of equity. If you are a newbie rental property investor, you may want to keep your day job as you learn the ropes of real estate investing. Start by doing research on healthy markets then establish realistic estimated profits and rent prices. Experts recommend that you invest enough in the properties so that you can have a positive cash flow. This way, you will not have to spend your income to run the business. Currently, it is difficult for newbie homebuyers to buy houses because most of the affordable ones are under negative equity. 18.8% of mortgaged homeowners in the U.S are underwater and cannot sell their homes without cash at the closing table. Because of this and expensive national rents, families have to rent at very high costs. The market may be ideal for landlords but not for rental property buyers. To engage in bidding wars, you will need a lot of money. Fortunately, some of the areas where properties are most expensive are highly demanded by renters. Be a smart buyer and buy properties in locations where both the rent and demand for rental houses are high. Properties in expensive locations have a high chance of appreciating in value and so long-term investment guarantees profit. If you do not have enough capital to buy rentals with cash, you should either invest in cheaper buildings or wait to buy. Do not go for prized properties, opt for working class neighborhoods instead where the rent is moderate. Before you buy rentals, plan your property management strategy carefully. Some property owners, especially those with handyman skills, may decide to run the entire business on their own, from emergency upgrades to tenant requests to signing leases. This strategy may seem cost-effective, but it is not beneficial for all rental owners. Some may have to hire property managers. Begin searching for rental property 3-6 months before you plan to buy. This timeframe will allow you to research the market and understand the current values. You can search online, or physically visit the units. If you do not have the time, hire an agent. When choosing a rental property, look for the qualities you might want for your own home. What appeals to you will appeal to renters. When you are an onsite homeowner, you will understand what it is like to live in your property and make the necessary improvements. Moreover, you will have access to affordable financing. Before you close on a home, invest in an inspection; and if upgrades are required estimate how much they will cost before you buy. Make the necessary upgrades immediately after buying for the safety of your tenants and to attract renters.

Chapter 22

Before Investing in Condos

E veryone wants a small source of income on the side and investing in a condo is a good option. Whether you are seeking to add a condo to your portfolio or just want to buy a second house to rent out, you need to consider a few things before investing in a condo. There are tighter restrictions imposed on financing condos than on detached homes. Lenders will usually ask for 20-25% down payment on investment properties. Other lenders will require that you live in the condo for not less than one year before you rent it out; otherwise you may have to pay a higher down payment. Ask your lender about any regulations concerning the financing of condos. Condos do not appreciate quickly compared to detached homes. However, the market and area are large determinants of this. Experts advise investors to think of condos as long-term investments in order to realize the highest return on their capital. Hold on to it for at least 5 years. Most condo associations have rental caps. This refers to the limit put in place by the HOA or condo board on the number of units that should be rented out. Make sure you know whether or not the unit you are buying can be rented out. The units of a building under litigation, for any defect, can barely be sold because getting bank financing for such condos is almost impossible. Even if you have all the money at hand, litigation is still something you should be cautious about. One major problem is a sign of many underlying issues. Special assessments are the fees that the HOA charges to cater for condo building repairs when the cost exceeds what is in the HOA account. These fees can cost a lot and they are mandatory. A HOA will, in most cases, have scheduled site inspections so as to determine the state of the grounds and building. They also have information about any recommended upcoming repairs. Ask your agent for reserve studies so that you will know of any upcoming repairs and what they may cost. HOA fees can be high so it helps to know what is covered. They cover sewer, water, garbage, grounds, a community center, security, exterior building maintenance, pool, etc. A HOA payment is more of a savings account for your house's maintenance. You can incorporate this payment into the rent amount. It will be easier to access the HOA through your agent before buying the condo. Ask for as many documents as possible from the HOA and read them. This will let you know how active and accessible it is. Buying a condo is one thing, renting it out is another. Check if all the units in the building are occupied and if not, find out why. Ask to know the rental rates in the building. Tenants are not easy to deal with. As a landlord, you have to address their issues carefully and in time. If you cannot do this, you might want to hire a property manager.

Chapter 23

Questions to Ask Yourself Before Buying a Fixer-Upper Property

A fixer-upper home is one that requires a significant or minor rehabilitation before being used. The repairs of a fixer-upper can mean a light cosmetic touch such as a new carpet or an intensive renovation such as a new roof. Fixer-upper houses can be a goldmine. However, properties like these are risky and you can lose a lot of money when you invest in them. See their advantages and disadvantages.

Advantages of Purchasing a Fixer-Upper

Less competition: nice homes are in high demand because that is what everyone is looking for. People want a move-in ready house and especially single-family houses. For multi-family properties, investors avoid buying a problem. When you decide to buy a fixer-upper, you eliminate most of the competition and you can easily find a deal, even in a crowded market. Forced appreciation: this concept can help you build immediate equity. Appreciation is a great generator of wealth in the real estate industry. With a fixer-upper property, you do not have to wait for years for the property to appreciate. After rehabilitation, a house can be worth much more than you bought and renovated it for. More cash flow: there is the potential of greater cash flow with fixer-upper properties because you buy them for way less than other houses in the neighborhood. You take out a loan on a cheap distressed house but rent it out for its new value. Unique financing options: most lenders will be hesitant to lend on fixer-upper properties. However, there is something you can do to buy a house without using much of your own money. To do this, look for a great deal and then find a private lender. After the seasoning period, refinance your house to a long-term mortgage.

Disadvantages of Purchasing a Fixer-Upper

Hidden expenses: there are the problems that you can see and then there are others that you will only discover once you start working on the houses. Estimating the exact amount that you will spend on rehabilitation is, therefore, difficult. Stress: fixing these homes is never an enjoyable process. There is a lot of drama, frustrations, and sometimes injuries, if you do the renovation yourself. If you hire a contractor, you should be ready to be disappointed occasionally. Out-of-pocket-costs: during the process of rehabbing a house, you will have a hard time sticking to your budget. The same goes for your timeline as well. You will find yourself spending more money than you thought you would and the project will take longer than you anticipated. Consequently, your ROI will be affected and the deal you thought was a great one may go down the drain.

5 Questions to Ask Before Investing in a Fixer-Upper

Should you even invest in these kinds of properties?

Despite the disadvantages discussed above, fixer-upper properties are still a good investment. Just take a look at the advantages. However, before you put in your money, ask these questions.

How Bad Is the Property?

Fixer-upper properties have different levels of severity. Some will only require a few thousand dollars while others will require a complete overhaul. Obviously, a property that needs little work is less risky. However, remember that if it requires less work, you will face more competition. Experts advise you to find properties that look like they need a lot of work but actually don't. A good example is a house that has a bad smell. Most investors will stay away from a house like this despite the fact that it is not hard to get rid of the smell. The same applies to bad roofs and an ugly exterior. Before you purchase a fixer-upper do a thorough evaluation.

Is It Worth It?

A fixer-upper is not automatically a great deal. In some cases, you will be better off buying a finished house. The cost of buying and rehabbing a house should not be more than (or even equal to) the cost of buying a similar finished house. If anything, the cost should be lower—that is what makes it a great deal.

Do You Have the Time?

It does not matter whether you hire someone to do the work or you do it yourself; the project takes time. You will have to drop by the house often to see to it that everything is going smoothly. Other times, you will have to do things on your own. Some projects end up taking years!

Do You Have the Skills?

Most investors interested in fixer-uppers plan to take care of the work themselves. This is highly encouraged, as long as it is on a small scale. You will save a lot of money and when you decide to hire people for future projects, you will be a great manager. However, you need to have the skills. Even if you do not have the skills, having the motivation and desire to learn will help you accomplish the project. You will be able to acquire the necessary skills and become a pro in no time.

Chapter 24

Why Passive Investing in Commercial Real Estate is a Smarter Strategy Than Single Family Rentals

Most real estate investors deal with single family houses. Having bought their own homes, this process is something they understand. Moreover, buying a second home is an attractive venture to the homeowner who has witnessed the gradual equity growth of their first home. This strategy is great. However, for the investor seeking to diversify in real estate, commercial real estate is a good way to build your portfolio. People do not realize it but having single family rentals is risky and tough. They come with many challenges such as:

No sustainable cash flow: many people purchase their single-family rentals with debt, hence little or no sustainable cash flow. Too much risk: there are great risks associated with owning single family rentals, especially when the property is leveraged. You may end up losing more than you invested. Lack of economies of scale: some large capital items such as cooling systems, driveways, roofs, and heating are used by one tenant. When the property incurs sudden capital costs your cash flow can be temporarily wiped out. Costly management: when you own single family rentals, you either hire someone to manage them for you (at a huge percentage of your income) or do it yourself (at a great opportunity cost). None of these scenarios is desirable. 100% market dependent: asset value is purely dependent on the overall market—it is not correlated to its profitability. Backyard reliant: investors will usually want to oversee their rental properties, so these rental homes have to be close to the investor's residence. Because of these challenges, single family rentals can hardly be justified as a component of a diversified portfolio. The Alternative: Passive Commercial Real Estate Investing

When investors understand how commercial real estate investment works, they will start moving away from single family rentals. An investor can directly own or operate commercial real estate. However, this is not easy as it requires specialization and a large amount of capital which may be a barrier to many investors. The better option is to be a limited partner with operating companies.

Here is why:

Asset value in correlation to NOI (net operating income): this means that the greater market does not necessarily determine whether you lose or gain money. The value of the property is correlated to its net operating income. The operator controls the destiny and it is not just about betting on the market. Co-investing with professionals: when you are ready to passively invest, you can look for sophisticated groups with great track records. Teaming up with veterans will help you mitigate some risk. Diversification: even in real estate investing, diversification is an awesome tool. Passive commercial real estate investing lets you choose a business plan, asset type, and geography with almost no limits.

Loss limitations: your liability as a limited partner is set at the investment amount.

Rationality: because commercial real estate has its competitiveness grounded in rationality, it is possible to reliably project the performance of a property. Single family rentals are not entirely bad. However, investors should view them as a starting point in real estate investing.

Chapter 25

How to Pick the Ideal Location for Investment Properties

A great location will ensure that you have an easy time attracting renters and give you high financial rewards. Although people will have a different definition of the best location, a great investment location should appeal to your target market and be profitable for you. In this chapter, you will learn about picking the best location for your investment. Real estate investment is like any other business. Therefore, demand and supply determine your profits. The ideal business should offer something that everybody wants or needs (high demand) and what it has to offer should not be easy to replicate (limited supply). A real estate investment can only be successful if the tenants have good jobs. Understand the job market of the area. Consider the following:

- The number of jobs; is the number increasing or decreasing?
- The median salary; is it increasing or decreasing?
- The types of jobs; low-paid laborers, high-tech or professional?
- Diversified jobs; a stable variety of job sources or 1-2 main industries?

Population Growth
People are always moving to locations with better jobs. They are also attracted by things like natural attractions, weather, local politics, and the price of housing.

The ideal location for real estate investing is one with an increasing population. The price/rent ratio is a great and easy way to evaluate the profitability of an area.

The rent/price ratio is determined by dividing the median price by median yearly rent. For example, if the median housing price in an area is $200,000 and the median yearly rent is $15,000, then the price/rent ratio is $200,000/$15,000 = 13.33. A location with a high rent/price ratio is not good for business.

Small Scale Location Criteria

Convenience

You have a better chance of success if you own properties where many people would like to live such as near a major economic center. Romance, in this case, is something that makes people emotionally attracted to a location. The decision on where to live is based on emotion.

Romance, depending on place, includes:

- Proximity to green spaces and parks
- Streets lined with trees
- Beautiful scenery, etc.

Romance differs with the location and you will have to physically visit a location to find out. Walkability has been associated with more price resilience and higher property appreciation. This is truer for metro areas than for rural areas and small towns. Everyone wants to live in a safe place. Avoid the worst areas, regardless of what they promise on paper. There are several sites online such as https://spotcrime.com/ and https://www.trulia.com/local/ which can give you the necessary statistics.

School Districts

Just like crime, you can find most information online, however, make sure you visit the area too and talk to the locals.

Public Transport

Proximity to public transit is an important factor in urban areas. Search Google to find public transit routes to help you in your research. Your attorney should share any CCRs (covenants, conditions and restrictions) when you are buying property. They are useful but can be limiting at times.

Local Laws, Finances, Taxes, and Infrastructure

The local government will influence your investment. Pay attention to eviction laws, property taxes, rental laws, licenses, municipal services, and rent controls.

Chapter 26
Real Estate Financing

"Free" real estate does not exist. Like any other commodity, you have to pay for it. This chapter aims at showing you how you can fund your investments. For you to invest without using much of your cash, you need to employ a number of strategies. You can even do some deals without using any of your money. Here are all the financing methods that you can use. Some investors opt for all cash when paying for their properties. This form of financing is probably the simplest and does not has major complications. It is, however, not an option for most investors. It is also not as profitable as leveraging. Since financing a deal is way more profitable than paying all cash, a lot of investors prefer financing with a conventional mortgage and a cash down payment. For most mortgages, you will need at least 20% down. This mortgage type is the most common among homeowners and has the lowest interest rates. There are several sources for conventional mortgage loans such as credit unions, mortgage brokers, and banks. These sources do not usually use their own capital but, instead, resell the loans to institutions backed by the government or borrow from another. When a source lends from its own funds, they become a portfolio lender. Portfolio lenders are flexible. You can enquire from your lending source whether or not they are portfolio lenders. The FHA (Federal Housing Administration) is a government program in the U.S that insures mortgages. Only homeowners who will live in the home are eligible. Since you cannot use it for a property that is purely for investment, you can buy a triplex or duplex and live in one unit. A 203K loan finances the purchasing of a distressed house together with the necessary repairs. You will still need to put some money down (3.5% or more). Like the FHA loan, you have to live in the property. The seller of the property can fund your purchase called owner financing, and in turn, you will be making monthly payments to them instead of a lending institution. This is only possible if the seller owns the property free-and-clear; otherwise, the home may face foreclosure. Hard money refers to financing received from a private individual or business. For short term loans, it may be beneficial but be cautious. Private money is almost the same as hard money but there is usually a relationship between the borrower and the lender. A private lender is less business-oriented and is just looking to get some return on their cash. Home Equity Line of Credit (HELOC) and Home Equity Installment Loan (HEIL) are products by lending institutions that let you tap into your primary home's equity to help you finance your investment property. An equity partner can help you finance a piece of property that you would otherwise not afford on your own. The partner can either fund the down payment or pay for the entire property. Commercial loans have higher fees and interest rates and different qualifying standards. It focuses more on the property than on the borrower income.

Chapter 27
How to Find Investment Properties

The potential for appreciation and profitability is one of the most important factors to consider. The general rule of thumb is that the monthly rent of a property should be at least 1% of its buying price. This means that you have to study the rent in the area, so you can estimate how much you should buy the property for. Simple landscaping means less upkeep both for you and your renters. You can expect your tenants to mow the grass but not all of them will be interested in taking care of huge plant beds or plant flowers. It is best to just find property that has low maintenance landscaping. Three or more bedrooms makes sense if the neighborhood has multiple people with children. It will be marketable to families and you will barely experience vacancies. Target three or more bedrooms. Remember, the more the bedrooms the more the rent. If your budget is low, you can only buy homes that require some work. Most of the homes you find will have out-of-style bathrooms, outdated kitchens, and other things that may need modern upgrades—and this is not that bad. You do not have to put a new bathroom or kitchen, unless it is really necessary. You might need to make minor repairs such as new floors but nothing major. When looking to rent to families, the neighborhood matters just as much as the home. Even after you find a nice neighborhood, be skeptical on the exact location of the home and the available amenities. It helps to find a property that is close to schools, parks, and shopping centers. When a home is this convenient, numerous people will be interested. Generally speaking, for rental real estate, property taxes are set at 2% of the gross value of the property. When you understand the property tax laws of your state, you do not have to guess the amount of taxes to pay. However, check the gross assessed value of the property before buying. The assessments are prone to being incorrect and you do not want any surprises later on. How you maintain a property will have a huge impact on the costs of future upkeep. You can always tell when a home has had little or no upkeep for a long time. When conducting your search, look for homes that have been cared for to avoid huge repair bills in future. Houses with a brick exterior are easier to maintain than those with steel sliding. A low-maintenance exterior will not require replacing—something that may cost you a lot of money. The biggest mistake you can make is to ignore a water problem, like a small pool in the backyard, because it does not seem serious. When you move in or turn the property into a rental, the problem is likely to get worse. Any trace of a water problem should be taken seriously. Make sure the drainage is excellent.

Chapter 28

Things to Look for When Buying Rental Property

Analyzing deals is one thing and buying property is another. In this chapter, you will learn how to get the best properties and deals. Your investing career does not begin with you getting a fat check. You will only get the check after you have applied multiple strategies. Your profits, however, are an entirely different story. They are either destroyed or made when you are buying. That is why experts say, "make profit when you buy". This is done by buying smart—at a price that will ensure profit when you apply investor techniques. Before you go searching for a property, outline your selection criteria. A selection criteria list is meant to guide you and keep you focused. It keeps you from getting distracted by whatever new trends or next big thing. The criteria list helps you narrow down your choices in the vast real estate market. When making your criteria list, there are a few items you may want to consider:

- Cap rate
- Neighborhood
- Property size
- Town
- Number of units
- Cash flow
- Property conditions
- Appreciation potential
- Lot size

You are the only one who knows what should or should not be in your property criteria. The kind of investment you are interested in will dictate your criteria.

The Rules of Investment Property

These rules help you to quickly evaluate the financials of a property. These rules should not be 100% relied on but you can, at least, use them to filter properties and see which one is worth evaluating further. Here are some of the rules:

- The 2% rule: your total rent per month should be roughly 2% of the buying price.
- The 50% rule: 50% of your income will go to expenses, excluding the mortgage payment.
- The 70% rule: only pay 70% of the after-repair value, minus the repair costs.

Where to Search for Real Estate Properties

The MLS (Multiple Listing Service): this is where many properties for sale are listed by various real estate brokers. They include sites such as redfin.com and realtor.com

The newspaper: buy your local newspaper and check the classified section.

Word of mouth: tell everyone that you are looking to buy a real estate property and even define your criteria.

Craigslist: this is one of the most popular sites in the world. You are sure to find many real estate deals here.

Outbound marketing: this involves making sellers come to you by direct mail, advertising, or any other marketing technique.

Loopnet.com: this is a market place for all kinds of commercial properties.

The Buying Process

The process of selling and buying real estate is not a simple one. Here are the steps you have to go through:

Step 1: choose your investment niche/strategy.

Step 2: clearly outline your selection criteria.

Step 3: come up with a method of financing; bank loan or cash.

Step 4: start looking for properties on the places discussed above.

Step 5: use your criteria list to filter the properties.

Step 6: make an offer to the seller.

Step 7: negotiate and come to an agreement with the seller.

Step 8: inspect the property and submit the required paperwork.

Step 9: sign the papers and wait for the paperwork to be recorded.

Chapter 29
The Guide to Making and Accepting an Offer on a Home

The purchase offer, on both sides of the transaction, is the initial formal communication leading to the final deal. In some cases, and especially in the largescale market, homebuyers are disadvantaged because they compete with other potential buyers for a limited number of houses. Formulating the offer is as much about what a potential buyer can offer as it is about the asking price. Placing an offer does not just involve saying how much you will pay. You should also state your expected closing date, prove your ability to pay, state your expectations of the seller, and how you want additional costs to be covered. When you submit an offer, you might have to give earnest money to show your seriousness.

What you should know:

When to place your offer: if the available properties are very few and potential buyers are many, the sooner you make your offer the better. Even if you place your offer immediately, there will be others to compete with. How much you should offer: the listing price will give you an idea on what the seller expects. However, an even bigger determinant is the real value of the house and the required repairs. If you have a real estate agent, he or she will show you a history of how much houses of the same size have been selling for. Your personal needs (what you are looking for) will also come into play. Submitting a contingent offer: if you are looking to sell your current home to get money for the new one, put it on the market first before you begin your search. Once you get a buyer, you can place an offer with home-close contingency. Competing with other buyers: competition among buyers is a big part of this process. Many of them hate to find themselves in a bidding war which could mean paying more or losing out. To stand out, write the seller a personal letter, include specific figures in your offer (as opposed to rounded off numbers) and be flexible. For Sellers: Accepting an Offer

Make sure your asking price and the condition of the home are attractive to buyers. Here is what you should do to make the home desirable and conduct a smooth and successful transaction. Set an offer deadline: when you set a short deadline, potential buyers will not have sufficient time to go hunting for another house. However, you need to study your market first. Knowing the limit: when setting the asking price, talk to your real estate agent to know how much the property is worth depending on recent sales. Factor in your needs as well. Getting the best offer: after receiving offers, you have to consider factors such as the buyer's financial security, the convenience of the timeline, and any other expenses and costs. Next, determine the deal's bottom line. Negotiating: even after finding the best offer, you can still negotiate some terms. As you negotiate, be cordial and consider the buyer's preferences. Accepting the offer: once you come to a mutual agreement with the buyer, you can now go ahead with the deal. A deal may still not go through even after negotiating. Additional information may come up, calling for more negotiation or having one party back out.

Chapter 30
Closing a Real Estate Deal

Closing a deal in real estate can be overwhelming. There are so many formalities and steps to follow. This chapter will help property buyers understand the closing process, from when the seller accepts your offer to when the home becomes yours. An escrow account is held by a third party for the two key parties in a transaction. Selling a home is a hectic process that might drag on for weeks. The third party holds documents and money associated with the transaction to avoid the possibility of the buyer or seller being ripped off. A title insurance and title search will offer a legal safeguard and peace of mind. You will be sure that once the property is yours, no one can claim it later. A title search involves examining public records to confirm the legal ownership of a property. Title insurance protects you as the holder from any financial losses should a defect in the title arise. Even if you are well-educated, you might have a hard time understanding the complex jargon in property documents, consult with an attorney. You do not really need to be pre-approved for a mortgage to close the deal, but it may hasten the process. It will also give you bargaining power because the seller will see your strong financial backing. Interest rates can be volatile. Even a small increase in interest rates can increase the amount you will repay and the repayment tenure significantly. Experts advise you to lock the rate in advance. This way, you will not leave your fate in the hands of market fluctuations. All the entities and services in this process will cost you money and the amount can be significant. If you don't know about this, you will be taken advantage of. Be willing to stand your ground and speak up. A thorough home inspection will let you know if the property has any problems and also allow you to see and feel the surroundings. If there is a problem, you are free to back out or talk to the seller, so they can fix it. A pest inspection is not the same as a home inspection. With a pest inspection, a specialist come to check and make sure that there are no carpenter ants or wood-destroying insects. Any pest issues, no matter how small, must be taken care of before the deal is closed. After the inspections, you can try to renegotiate the offer depending on the cost of any necessary repairs. Alternatively, ask the seller to cater for the repairs. Ensure that contingencies are removed in writing. Make sure you know the approval process and do what is required by the stated dates. In addition to the earnest money, you have to add more money into escrow. The original earnest money will definitely become part of the down payment. Make sure all the payments required at various times are arranged or the deal is cancelled. Before signing the final papers, go and check out the property again. Any necessary repairs should have been made and there should be no new problems. Paperwork is a very critical step. Read everything even though it appears to be complicated and consult on what you do not understand.

Chapter 31

DIY Landlord: Your Guide to Managing Your Rental

L earn about the advantages and disadvantages of being your own rental property manager and a few useful tips on making it a success. Will your personality type allow you to maintain a professional relationship with the tenants? If your tenant damages something, pays their rent late, or does something wrong, can you, unemotionally, apply your legal rights? As a DIY landlord, you will have to deal with tough issues like evicting tenants and demanding rent among others. In every jurisdiction, there exists legal and legislative structures to protect both the landlord and the tenant. As a DIY landlord, you need to understand the Acts and legislation. If possible, take a short property management course. Make sure you also have standard documents and agreements such as bond lodgment forms and lease agreements. As a property manager, one of your most important tasks will be rent collection. Set a clear process to be followed and ensure that the rent is paid in full by the required date. Do not take partial payments. If a tenant fails to pay their rent, send them a written reminder. From the 10th to 14th day, you can start formal proceedings. Follow all the steps carefully and do not harass your tenant. Once in a while, you will find yourself looking for a new tenant after the old one moves out. The leasing process involves these important steps:

Advertising: this involves making a multitude of people want to live in your property because then, you can select the perfect tenant. Borrow advertising ideas from fellow property owners.

Receiving enquiries: be accessible and act professional in this step.

Tenant screening: make a list of questions and do not shy away from asking them. Interview the potential tenants by phone and in person, then do a background check.

Application acceptance: when you find the perfect tenant, accept their application immediately before they are grabbed by another landlord. Your property should be up to par in landscaping and move in ready. There are rules in each state concerning the number of times a property should be inspected per year. Know the rules of your state and adhere to them. Remember to keep photographs and records. As a DIY landlord, always seek to know what is happening around you. When increasing rent, be careful to abide by the laws of your state and the terms of the lease. DIY landlords, in most cases, do not understand tenant rights when it comes to repairs and maintenance. There are repairs that are considered urgent. If the tenant pays for these, they have a right to ask for the money back from you. Have maintenance workers on call who can attend to urgent repairs. A DIY landlord should be readily available, so you can take care of issues as they come up. Everything can be overwhelming and frustrating especially if you have another job. Have someone who can help when you are unavailable. The relevant systems and technology will make the management process easier. Keep all the records associated with the property safely and in order. Management costs are deductible and if you claim them, you can lower your taxable income.

Chapter 32

Dealing with Problem Tenants

There are all kinds of tenant issues and as a landlord, you will have to deal with a few of them at one point or another. In this chapter, you will learn how to deal with common tenant issues without losing your head. Is the rent late, again? Are other tenants bombarding you with messages about loud music or a foul smell? When an issue with a tenant arises, avoid getting emotional and take care of the problem immediately. Before you begin diffusing the situation, there are things you need to consider. Every state has its ordinances and laws. Understand your responsibilities and rights, the rights of the tenant, eviction, and notices procedures. Talk to an attorney (recommended) or go through the Department of Housing website of your state. Your lease agreement should clearly state the policies, regulations, and rules of the property. The tenant should get a copy when they are moving in. Document your procedures and policies for dealing with a tenant issue, notices, warnings, forms of communication, and the expected response time. Document your interaction with the tenant. You and your staff should know procedures and policies. Make sure you understand types of incident reports, tenant warnings, and termination notices. Maintain professionalism, regardless of whether the tenant does or not. Tenants may come with all kinds of stories; hard, sad or good. Be empathetic but unwavering and firm as far as your policies are concerned. Discuss the details of the problem with the tenant alone, not a significant other or family member. Issues like hoarding or late payments are a violation of your policies but they are also not easy for the tenant. Handle things with confidentiality and be careful if you have to share information with the rest of the tenants. Call the police if you think anyone is in danger. Even professionalism should not come before safety. Contact the relevant authorities if illegal activities are involved then follow the eviction procedure.

Your local laws will give you an idea of how to serve a notice and make sure you serve the correct one. The most common notices include:

- Nonpayment of rent notice
- Cure or quit notice
- Unconditional quit or vacate notice

Common Problem Tenants and How to Respond

Late-paying or non-paying tenant: if rental policies are clearly outlined, make sure you follow through with the repercussions. If the tenant completely fails to pay rent, serve a Nonpayment of Rent Notice. Noisy and disruptive tenant: document the complaint you receive from neighbors. Talk to the tenant and if the problem persists, serve a Cure or Quit Notice. Property-destroying tenant: write to the tenant asking them to repair the damage or fix it yourself and send them the bill. If this does not work, serve a Cure or Quit Notice. Illegal activities tenant: call the police or the relevant authorities as soon as you get the evidence. Property abandoning tenant: talk to an attorney so you can know what to do with their personal items.

Chapter 33
1031 Exchange and Rental Properties

Among the many advantages of rental properties are favorable tax benefits. With a 1031 exchange, you can sell your rental homes and defer the taxes. However, failure to adhere to the numerous rules and regulations of the 1031 exchange, you may receive a huge tax bill. A 1031 exchange is a transaction in real estate involving two similar properties; one being bought, and another being sold within a specific time frame. Restrictions surrounding the 1031 exchange are so many and the IRS does not state them clearly. Some of the basic principles assert that the property should be used for business, be held for not less than a year, and that the new property should be found in 45 days and purchased in 180 days. If you meet all these requirements (and others), you can sell your rental property and not pay the recaptured depreciation or taxes on the profit. If you sell a rental house, you are required to pay taxes on the profit and also pay recaptured depreciation. The IRS allows you to depreciate a rental house because, according to them, the structure's lifespan is limited, and its value decreases yearly. The depreciation amount can be deducted from your taxes yearly. Nevertheless, if you sell the property for an amount that is higher than the depreciated value, you will be required to pay back all the taxes you saved. Many types of real estate properties qualify for the 1031 exchange according to the IRS. This includes any business property such as an office building, a manufacturing facility, or a store. You can also use some investment buildings such as rental properties for a 1031 exchange. The IRS states that you cannot use a fix and flip for a 1031 exchange. However, if you do not fix and flip constantly, you can use a 1031 exchange but only if you meet these set guidelines:

- You have to rent out the property for not less than one year after you fix it
- If it has been rented for less than one year, you can neither list nor sell it

You must use a qualified intermediary to oversee the transaction. Anyone associated or related to the TP (Tax Deferred Exchange) cannot be an intermediary. The intermediary is responsible for holding the money after the first property is sold and using it to purchase the new property. If you do not want to pay taxes in a 1031 exchange, all the money you receive after selling the first property has to be used in purchasing the new property; otherwise, you may be required to pay taxes on the remainder amount. In the title of the new house, you have to use the same name that was in the old property's title. Instead of selling your original property then buying the replacement, it is possible to purchase the latter first, then sell the former.

Chapter 34
Mistakes Inexperienced Landlords Make

According to many people, being a landlord does not seem like a very difficult job. However, you need to think like a business professional. Many new landlords are likely to make these mistakes and end up losing sleep, time, and even money. Every new landlord wants to get a tenant in as fast as possible; but you will not be helping your case if you do things in a rush and fail to check the credentials of your tenant. Have a rental application form to help you gather enough information and get a credit report. Take your time and go over references from former employers and landlords. Let nothing pressure you into making an uninformed decision. Before you close on a deal, do your due diligence to know whether or not you will still be able to pay the mortgage even when you have vacant units. If you do not analyze your cash flow properly, you may end up having the property foreclosed and have your finances ruined. A properly maintained property attracts tenants. While deciding how much rent to charge, factor in regular maintenance costs such as carpet cleaning, painting, etc. If something happens and you have to make a huge one-time repair, be ready to take money out of your own pocket or the business to cater for it. Rental property investing is a business and if you want to make any profit you will have to think of it as such. The expenses and deposits should have separate bank accounts. Have an elaborate bookkeeping system and talk to a tax professional about your taxes. Promises do not count in business. Be legally protected by ensuring that every tenant sign a lease agreement when they are moving in. They should clearly understand the terms stated in the contract. When conducting the screening interview, you should be careful to avoid the risk of being sued. It is illegal to reject a tenant's application based on religion, race, marital status, family status, etc. Your rental property is your responsibility. Conduct regular checks to see the condition of your property. Be careful, though, not to violate your tenant's privacy. Let them know you are stopping by because you can get sued. Your property must meet health and safety standards at all times. If you do not do as the law requires, your tenants may get a reason to violate the lease agreement terms, receive compensation for injury/ damage, or sue you. Start the eviction proceedings once it is legally possible; failure to do this can cost you a lot. Talk to an eviction attorney immediately if you do not know what to do or what your rights are. If the lease agreement states that breaking rules will attract a penalty, enforce the penalty. Uphold the standards you have set, and your tenants will follow suit. All interaction with a tenant should be documented in writing. You will see how important they are if you ever go to court.

Chapter 35

The Definitive Guide to Using Seller Financing to Buy Real Estate

Seller financing is one of the most common methods that people use to invest with little or no money down. It is an old method, but its popularity has been declining over the years recently. However, it is still a good method as you will see in this chapter. As the name suggests, seller financing is where the financing comes from the seller. The person selling you the property takes the role of the bank. When the legal ownership is transferred to you, you send the payments directly to the seller instead of the bank. After agreeing on the price, the seller will ask for a down payment and set an interest rate on the remainder amount, duration of payment and the monthly amount you will be paying him. The "due on sale clause" is the biggest downside of seller financing. It is a part of just about every mortgage. It gives a bank legal rights to demand for the full loan payment at once, if the home is sold. Therefore, if the seller has an existing mortgage, seller financing may not work. However, this clause only gives a bank the right, but the bank may decide not to demand the payment and they might even agree with the arrangement. The best option is to just find a free-and-clear owned property.

The Benefits of Seller Financing

Ease of financing: seller financing spares you the trouble of using a bank—which is great for people who cannot get a mortgage.

Low or no down payment: depending on how you negotiate with the property owner, you may end up putting very little or nothing down.

Creativity option in structuring the deal: seller financing leaves room for creativity, unlike banks which have rigid rules. You can negotiate practically everything and end up with an awesome deal.

Buy "un-financeable" property: when a property is in very poor condition, you may be unable to get traditional financing. In this case, seller financing comes in handy.

Will not appear on your credit report: it is highly unlikely that a seller would sign up with a credit reporting agency to report the debt. Many sellers would prefer monthly payments over a long period of time instead of one large check. Here are some of the reasons which would make sellers opt for seller financing.

- Monthly income
- Better ROI
- Spread out taxes
- Lack of an alternative selling option

If the seller does not own the property free-and-clear, he or she can finance a fraction of the deal and the other part will be financed by a traditional lender. There are three easy ways to get seller financed deals:

- Ask
- Direct mail
- Look for keywords on websites

Draw Backs and Risks

There are three major concerns associated with the seller financing method:

- The due on sale clause
- Higher interest rates
- Fewer potential properties

Seller financing allows you to acquire properties without using bank services. However, this is no reason to overpay for houses. Make sure you get a great deal.

Conclusion

I f you have ventured into real estate investing, that is one of the best decisions you have ever made so far. Many people, some of them your friends and family, may never make such a decision and take charge of their financial fate. However, since you have chosen this path, you now hold great power; and you have heard, "with great power comes great responsibility". You may not feel successful now and there is no problem with that. The habits discussed below will make you a successful investor if you apply them. One of your greatest responsibilities as an investor in real estate is to be an effective manager of your portfolio. It does not matter whether you manage your own property, or you have hired a property manager, you are a manger. Owning rental property is never a walk in the park. There are many issues that you may have to encounter such as bad property managers, bad employees, economic depressions, natural disasters, among many others. Learn to properly manage your property and your finances. Increasing your rental property income is another task. This does not just refer to increasing the rent. To accomplish this, you should always rent out your property at the market rate. You will lose out on a lot if you decide to offer below market rent. Renting too high may also be a problem. Vacancy is one of the main cash flow killers and you will experience it a lot if your rent is too expensive. This does not mean that you become a penny pincher. Your tenants also have a right to enjoy the property. However, you can cut costs in many ways. For instance:

- Transfer some utility payment responsibilities to the tenant (electricity, garbage, water)
- If your property tax bill is too high, challenge it

- Try getting better insurance rates
- Apply water-saving techniques
- Use energy efficient appliances
- Look for vendors who will offer lower rates for longer contracts
- Switch to fewer (but larger) garbage pick ups
- Also, don't forget to compare insurance companies for your rentals.

These simple strategies will help reduce your expenses. They may appear minor but in the long run, they have huge financial benefits. A plan in real estate investing is crucial. Not having one is like driving aimlessly without a map across the country. Make sure you have a plan and a goal. If you already have one, carry it out. If possible, go back and check your goals everyday then monitor your progress every month. Your plan will not remain the same, it will keep changing as your career advances; and that is fine. Just follow through with it. It does not matter the level of your success, you have a duty to give back. There are many ways to do this but try giving back financially and educationally. Share with others what your investing journey has taught you. Join a community of investors (from all levels) so you can all learn, share and grow as a family. Your story might make a change in someone's life.

www.ingramcontent.com/pod-product-compliance
Lightning Source LLC
Chambersburg PA
CBHW071243170526
45165CB00003B/1222